Behind all the tears

Behind all the tears

a poetry collection

RASHA MOHAMED

ACKNOWLEDGEMENTS

Thank you, to the ones who made me laugh. But more importantly, to the ones who made me cry. To the ones who were gentle. But more importantly, to the ones who gave me hell. To the ones that touched my heart, but more importantly, to the ones who pained my soul. Because without you, the tears would not have fallen, and the words would not have woven together this book.

Thank you, to the ones *Behind All The Tears.*

CONTENTS

DO THEY REALLY LEAVE US?

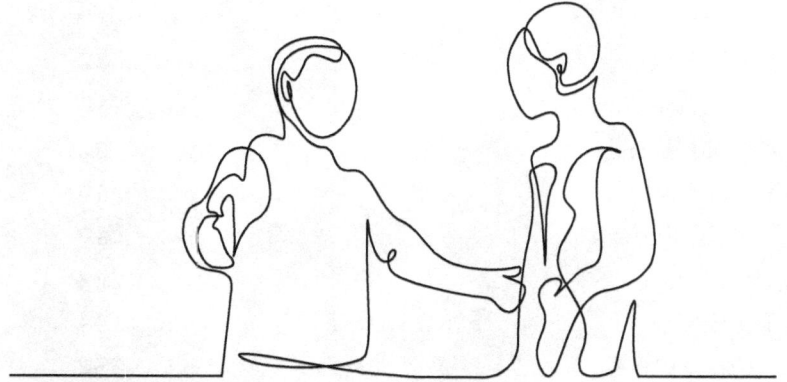

They leave us
But
do they really leave us?

They leave the world
But
they don't leave our hearts

They leave their bodies
But not the characters they embodied

Push the button
It all starts to end

They return the gifts
they were blessed with
Gently back
into the places they rose from
Wrapped in silk
they descend back
to where it all began

In the finest grains and dirt
Slides between their fingers

Warm
Protected from the storm

Preserved
Every bone in every cell that rose now falls

They sink into peace
Plummet into the light
Into the piercing breeze

Cold enough to breathe and feel
Their last breath
Last sight
Last scent
Last taste
Last touch

They rest their eyes
Clear their minds
Leave their memories behind

They shed their fears
Release their dreams

No inhibitions now
No who, what, when, where, or how

The alarm now rings
The green light shines
The gates open wide

Silence

Like the sound of the Sahara
Like the silky waters of the Red Sea
Like a child in the womb

Silence

Deeper now
Ears, they don't hear a sound
Or footsteps above ground
Or the wind racing
Raindrops falling
Infants crying
Lovers moaning
Engines roaring
Heels stomping
Waves crashing

Silence

They rest
In peace, they indulge
They are the lucky ones
Chosen from the masses
Handpicked from the fields

From the rest, they shine
They saw
Were never blind

They will remain loved
Remembered
They will be missed
as they rise
to their new shelter

And when our eyes rest at night
we reunite
And relive every moment we spent
Every feeling felt
Before they left us
But
do they really leave us?

THE APOCALYPSE

What if
the light at the end of the tunnel is an oncoming train?

What if
there's no rainbow after the rain?

What if
you don't learn from your lessons
or survive the present?

What if
there's no gain after the pain
and the insane are those who reign?

Will you remain?

What if
this is the apocalypse?

❈

ONE TEAR

We fight so hard
to keep our tears hidden
Years, we were taught and warned
that tears are forbidden

The child falls and scrapes her knees
She cries, she pleas
For a helping hand she reaches
But she must be strong
Perfect, can never be wrong

A look into her mother's eyes
she sees that she's in the wrong
The tear slowly returns to its duct
in slow, slow, slower motion

She grabs her knee
in agony
In pain, she looks up at the tree

Was it the inanimate object's fault
that injured her with its bark?
Or was it her own flesh
who's at fault?

She looks down at her scrapes
Then up at the tree
Finally, she decides
for the first time
and for the rest of her life

that she is in the wrong
She must be strong
and always move on

So she lives
Her future begins
No tears
No sorrow
Just blame
Heart Hollow
With every sad encounter
she screams inside her soul louder
On her journey
all she needs sometimes
is to rest on a gurney

But she moves on
Then she hears that boys are also told not to cry
That they can't be vulnerable
At one point she felt she was a guy
Just like them she didn't share her feelings
She hung out with the boys
She saw herself in them
Hiding behind their shields
Racing in the fields
Batting
Throwing
Jumping
Fighting
To hide what's inside

To be strong men
with pride

She belonged with them
They belonged with her

Because they were both taught
that feeling
Crying
Hurting
Sharing
Was for the weak
But she and the boys wanted to reach out
To be heard
To be seen
To be loved
To be touched

And for the first time they were
Heard
Seen
Loved
Touched

Their shields broke in pieces
to the ground
Each brick of each wall that they built
came tumbling down
Each dam that protected them
collapsed

They became
Bare
Naked
Free
When their first tear
Released

Just one tear
One eye
One duct

Slowly descends down one cheek
Slides next to one nostril
Reaches the side of the lip
Southbound

The tongue now tastes it
A foreign object
Unrecognizable
No frame of reference
of this strange fluid
Filled with sorrow
Pain
Fear
Hurt
The girl and the boys
swallowed this drop of liquid

For the first time
They were set free

No pain
No shame
A lifetime of guilt they built
Learned
Fed
Taught

It was all they knew
So they're not to blame
for the false lessons
of which they were framed

Because all it took
was that one tear
down one cheek

The girl ran back to the tree
Told it,
You're not the boss of me
It's not my fault
That I fell
And I will fall again
I will not be shamed
To express
To cry
To scream
To feel

Then she saw another tear drop
from her other tear duct
The boys too

Not one tear, but two
Now they are complete
They live in peace

And it all started
with one tear
down one cheek

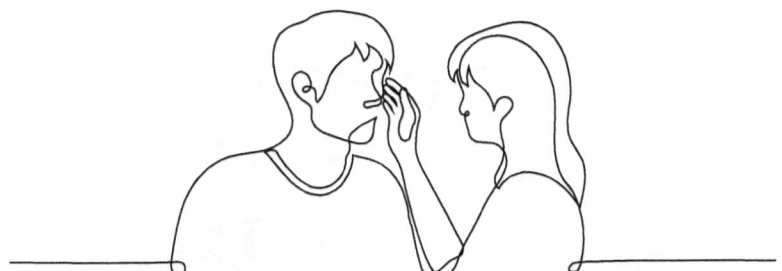

THE RETURN OF FEAR

After all the tears
The years
of suffering
recovering
and sorrow
You returned with fears
Hollow
Who do you think you are?
God?
Well consider me
an atheist
a convert
Because I won't revert
to being your servant

HOW TO STAY SAFE

You want to know how to stay
Safe
Comfortable
Protected?

Always say, *No*

But you'll also stay
Scared
Stupid
Disconnected

And never
Ever
Grow

❧

AFib

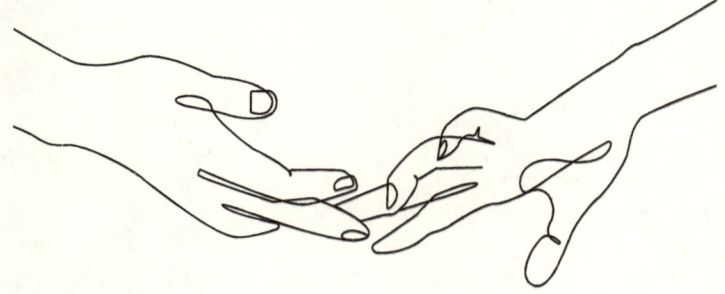

Atrial Fibrillation
A condition
Unregulated heartbeat
and rhythm

90 bpm to 140 bpm
160 to 110
It jumps then descends

AFib
A condition of the heart
when electrical signals
cause heartbeats to pause

This condition can be managed
However
With medication
Cardioversion
Ablation
Where electrophysiologists
burn or freeze the heart's electrical signals
that cause scarring of the heart

Did you hear that?
Scarring of the heart to help
AFib patients longer live

Scarring of the heart
to regulate the heartbeat
Scarring that remains for a lifetime
so one can live the time of their life

But if scars of the heart
can help one live
Then why
does one die
when one feels the scars
of being unloved?

How do we manage or cure
heartache from heartbreak?

Propitiously
modern science has discovered
a method to treat cardiac problems

Unfortunately
there are no medical devices
or a physician who advises
how to treat the pain when one feels like
their heart is broken
Not by an injury, old age
or genetics
But by the one whom you've handed your heart to
The one who caused you to skip
while your heart skipped a beat

The one whose brightest star
Spica was shared with Libra
Born 15,000 years ago in Egypt
Virgo

15,000 years later
Spica no more shines
Virgo's fields of wheat run dry
Libra's scales of justice cry
Hearts no longer skip
Blood in veins no longer flood
No medical device
Nor constellation
Ablation
Cardioversion
Medication
can restart their heartbeat
Resuscitation

Two Broken Hearts
In the cardiac trauma center of an infirmary
In separate beds
Arms stretched
Fingers touch

They gaze in each other's souls
as their souls prepare to soar

A herd of angels in white coats
fly with stethoscopes
They measure the beat of their hearts
Vital signs plunged

The touchscreen monitor with bright numbers
and zig zag graphs

screams
BEEP BEEP
Physicians warn
STAND CLEAR

Zap 1000 voltages
BEEP BEEP BEEP

Rises the atrium
Faster than a Hennessey venom
BEEP BEEP BEEP BEEP

Zap
STAND CLEAR
2000 voltages

BEEP BEEP BEEP BEEP BEEP

Zap
STAND CLEAR
3000 voltages

Silence

0 bpm
No beep
No sound
No zap
But none of this they feel

For when their eyes close
their souls arose
They secretly knew
that ablation
Cardioversion
Medication
Defibrillation
Does not treat their condition
For a Broken Heart is a heart broken
Into bright crystals, love tokens

They gaze closer
into each other's eyes
as their eyelids close

Their souls ascend
to continue the dance
they once began

No background noise
of beeps
cries
white coats
Their million tries
to salvage their hearts that rest
in cardiac arrest

They look down from the heavens
as their vessels rest soulless below

Goodbye, they wave
For tomorrow, they crave
and now, they wait
for another day they shall spend
in their pure, reborn hearts
perfectly designed
by the Divine

They continue their journey
in this new place
where she reads him Rumi
as his head tenderly rests on her lap
Where he writes her poems
that make her smile, cry and laugh
As he softly gazes into her eyes
that inspire every letter of every word he writes

Their heartbreak is now unbroken
Their love reawakens

True, they have been evicted physically
But in reality, spiritually, and in eternity
their hearts shall live in love, perpetually

Finally, they have learned
that exists treatments that manage AFib

Equally, they have learned
that treatments exist
to unbreak a Broken Heart
Not with medication
Cardioversion
Ablation
Defibrillation

Not with open heart surgery
But with an Open Heart
that chooses Love over fear
an open heart
that never shuts or disappears

An open heart
that believes
with conviction
that just like AFib
a broken heart can be mended

An open heart that believes with conviction
That the most significant thing in life
is Love

✖

THE SAVIOR

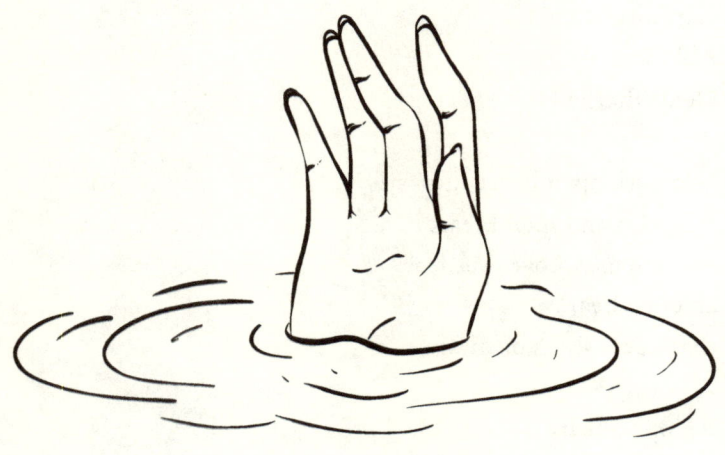

In the desert
Who will save you?
Who will hand you H_2O?

In the fire
Who will put you out?
Who will pull you out?

In the water
When it's your last breath
Who will delay your death?

Will it be you?
Will you save you?
Look in the mirror
Look up to your savior

AN OLD FRIEND

For me, to hold a pen again
is like meeting an old friend
Swept away in the desert sky
That writes between the cosmic lights

I was lost without my friend
the pen

It missed being touched
Held
Felt
Bitten
Dropped
And picked up again
My pen
To do what it does best
To write
is what it missed

Gracefully it dances on the lines
Twists and turns
Sways its hips back and forth
Stands up straight
With confidence and looks ahead

As it takes steps with precision
Written perfection

And now the empty paper is being filled
With blue ink

Red, blue, black, it writes free
With every color that our cones can see

But what we don't see
is exactly where it wants you to be

The pen
My friend
Creates words that are mute
Yet, they speak so loud
Like 10,000 amps at a concert enthralling the crowd

As it pours its heart out
As it speeds its steps
As it amplifies its letters
Intensifies its cases
Multiplies in spaces

It's not those words that are the loudest, strongest, fastest
Because those squiggles on paper are words written
But those
Those are not
Those are not
What it wants

You to read
You to see

You can't see the words that the pen wants you to feel
To touch
To Hear
To Breathe

This pen
It wants you to know that no matter how hard you try
to read between the lines
You'll never understand the unwritten words written just
with your eyes

Why not,
Because, said the pen
The unwritten words that I don't write are only read
with your heart
Not your eyes

So close your eyes
Open your heart
Listen to the sound of nothing
And breathe in the spirit

Close your eyes and realize
that the words that the pen writes
are only scribbles that jump, loop, or twist
in cursive or print

But between each word written
is the gem
In the empty silence
and the deserted space
is the meaning of the surrounding space

�֎

YOU ARE WHOLE

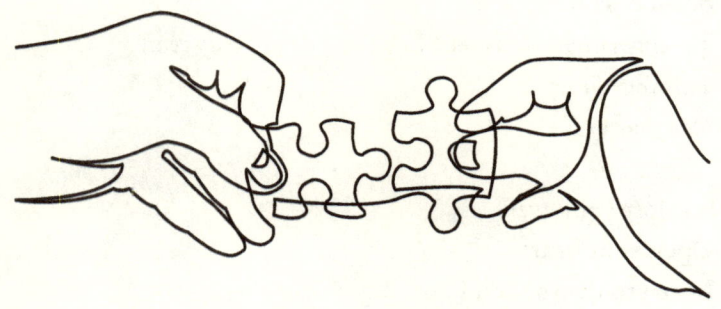

There is thunder in the silence
and warmth in the wind

There is light in the darkness
and sadness in happiness

There is hemorrhage under the gauze
and air that is caged

There is breath under water
and oxygen inflamed

There is company in solitude
and whispers in the storm

There are opposites who are identical
and fear on the battlefield

There are snakes that give warm hugs
and hugs that are sneaky

There are animals that are humane
and humans who are animals

There is pain in healing
and healing in grieving

There are secrets made public
and publicity with secrecy

There are thorns that protect roses
and roses that beautify thorns

There's this
And there's that
We see this
And feel that
We hear this
And touch that

We are all this
We are all that

We are whole
You are whole

�֎

CALL THE SHOTS

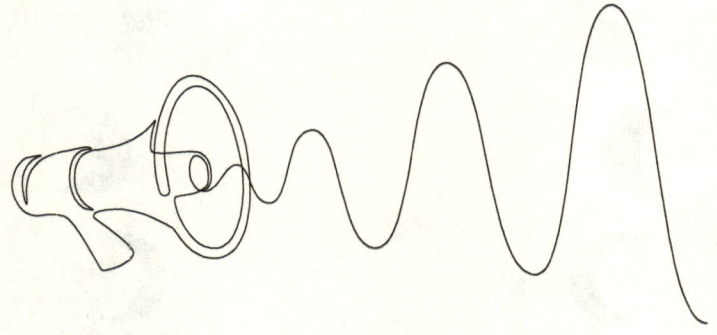

Who calls the shots
before the shot clock
hits zero?

Is it God
Your hero?
You're His apostle on the ground
But you're getting out of bounds

Get back in the game
and call your own shots

Because after foul six
there ain't no more tricks

❀

THE RETURN

She came back
Although I put her to sleep
She came back
Crying
Terrifying
Full of vengeance
Ready to attack
I thought I locked her up
I did
She found the key
Unshackled, she liberated herself
From the oppression
Depression
Obsession
She's free now
She's me now

THE BRIDGE

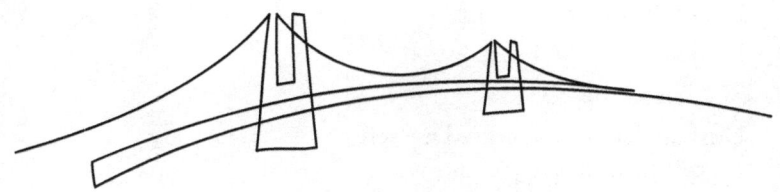

Chasing dreams
From the West to the Middle East
From Africa to North America
From the Nile to forest fires

A void I try to fill
A disease that makes me ill
Like fireflies, my dreams I can't grab
But I keep chasing
when my heart is stabbed
I look around, everyone seems ok
But are they?
Like me, afraid?
Of what?
I'm not sure
The past, the present, the future

I continue my journey
No itinerary
I make pit stops on the way
to write, dream, and play
Then I realized
that what I was searching for
was beneath my eyes

Obsessed with my dreams
My windshield wasn't clear
I was driving too fast
to get to the other side
Neglected the bridge I traveled by

No matter how high, wide, narrow, or extended
or how perilous the suspension
it took me to the destination
On my journey, it led the way
Held me tight, so I don't go astray

It wrapped its hands around me tight
Said, *Hey, it'll be alright*
I'm taking you through your fears and the darkness
It wiped my tears, their saltness
Gave me confidence
Resilience

A hemi engine, well designed
Pushed me forward
Power machine, revitalized
Eight cylinders inline
On the outside, unpaved roads
Bumps, potholes
On the inside,
Smooth silence
Peace, nonviolent

No fists across the face
Shoulders displaced
No shoving to the ground
Dignity unfound
No shame
No blame
No silencing the brain

No blood
No escaping the flood
of the illusion of love

Pushing you in the corner
Feeling like a foreigner
in a place called home
Turned into a storm
of goblins, witches and monsters
Humans engulfed with anger
Masks conceal what's under
Beneath the smiles on their face
Their ugly unrevealed
No tranquility or grace
Monsters of the night
Poking you to fight

A battle unexpected
You jumped in unprotected
No sword or shield
Your organs drenched in fear
But the fear within
rushed the adrenaline
Through your veins and arteries
the blood rushed to your feet

Fists up without gloves
Protect you from the punch
Their speed, accuracy, coordination
Coming at you like Foreman

47

Intimidation

Charged like Tyson
They clench their fists
Like Ali's snapping jab
Ribs about to crack
You neutralized and grabbed
They punched you to the floor
The crowd cheered, *T-K-O*

You lay in the ring
Did they win?
Ten, nine, eight, seven
About to zero
You failed as a hero

Life flashed before your eyes
Recalled the fights that won the prize
But now you're on the floor
Paralyzed
Weak
Demonized
Ostracized

The voice in your head whispered, *You're not dead*
Your energy began to flow
Your mind swung open its doors

Your feet started moving
Your eyes looked around

No voices, no sound
They wanted to keep you down
Your face to the ground
You pushed and shoved
Flew right off the floor
Glanced to see who's there
Monsters, goblins, witches everywhere

It hit you in the face
The reality of this place
Dark, evil, infected, toxic
Cold, like the Arctic

Exit sign
A door across the hall
called your name from afar
Come to me, I'll keep you safe
There's a bridge out there
that can take you to a better place

A cosmic energy tugged at you
Fear in your gut, it was all so new
Never from a fight you flew
But this time around
they treated you like a clown
They booed and threw filthy food

But you kept a straight path on your bloody feet
Like a soldier, it's your creed
It led you to the bridge that was always there
With open arms, no despair

They thought you forfeited and escaped the fight
Little did they know that you chose to choose
Your battles
So you can win the war

When you looked in the mirror and decided,
This battle isn't worth it
Your strength and courage within
helped declare your win
You used your intellect and reasoning
Your judgement, no feelings

Your mind was the weapon
Analyzed the situation
Led you to the bridge
Pushed you off the edge

No more reasons to fight
The bridge ahead
Infinite
Exquisite
You're the only one to fill it
with dreams and imagination
You walk to your destination

You learned from the fight
The truth you hid from the light
The reality of your plight
Your empire cracked but didn't crumble
You didn't fall, only stumbled

You discovered the how, the who
Wiped the fog off the windshield
Cruised through
The weak, they
The hero, you

You laughed
Realized
This is how it's supposed to be
It wasn't the destination that made you happy
It was always the bridge
The bridge
That set you free

NOBODY CARES

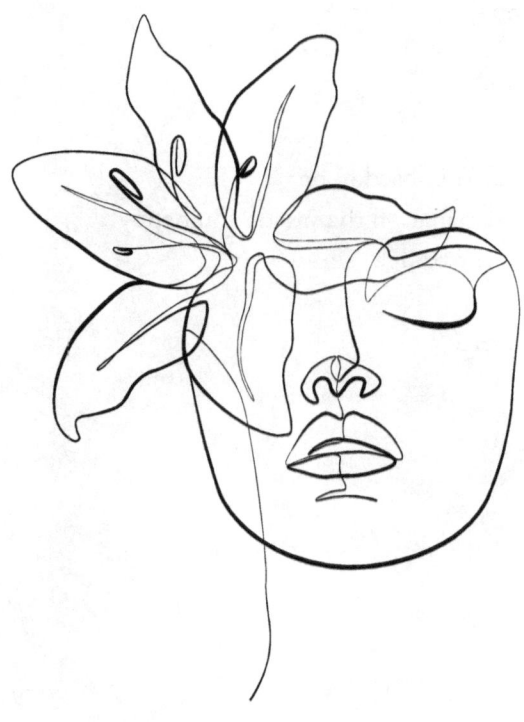

Nobody cares
Whether you live or die
They laugh in your face
Turn around and they lie

Nobody cares
If you fail or succeed
When you fall
they'll question your creed

Nobody cares
about the money you make
When it's all gone
they'll pound you like cake

Nobody cares
where on the ladder you are
Stay on the bottom
in case you fall

Nobody cares
Where you're going on vacation
Bermuda, Jamaica, or Fisherman's Wharf
You're the only one enjoying it
So just keep it to yourself

Nobody cares
who wins the elections
Republican, Democrat, boring, or funny
People will still die and go to bed hungry

Nobody cares
about your status or post
Get offline
Stop feeling lost

Nobody cares about your surface
What's under is more beautiful

Remove the mask
Reveal the flaws
Quit the shame
Live your truth

�֎

TELL YOUR KIDS

You won't tell your kids
The shit that you did
Yet
You expect them to be perfect
To worship your greatness

They grow up wanting to emulate you
If they only knew
what attention you drew
selling crack, guns, and popped a few
The system invited you
Popo chasin' you

I don't judge the past
nor the present

Tell your kids your flaws
Tell 'em you ain't perfect

Tell 'em you changed your path
Of you, they'll be proud

Write them a letter
Tell them you're better

Tell your kids
The shit that you did

✖

QWERTY

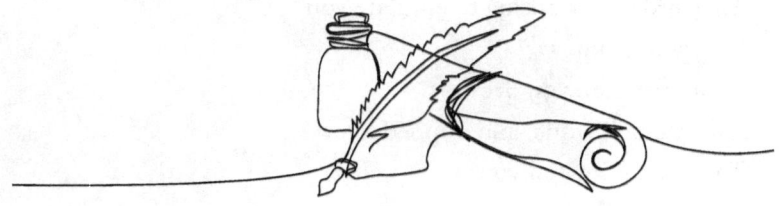

A board of keys
from A to Z
Out of characters, we create
Love and hate

The impossible
Unimaginable
Despicable

The case that's upper
and the lower

Millions of images we teach
From the beauty
to the beast

Papyrus from you to me
QWERTY
From A to Z

EMPTY CONVERSATIONS

Artificial smiles
What is on their minds?
The thrill?
Or a void to fill?
A walk on the boardwalk
with Fendi, Gucci, and Balmain
A fix of dopamine
Serotonin
Adrenaline
Unintelligent
Still
Empty conversations
Artificial smiles

CONTROL

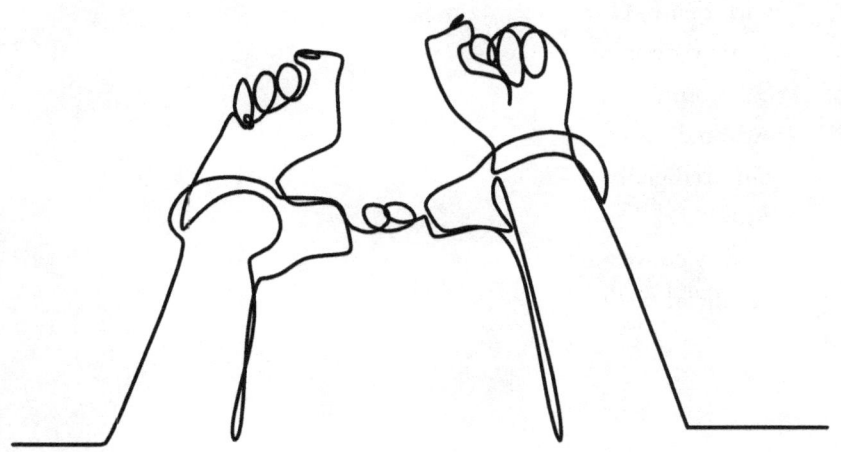

What is CONtrol?
  It's a CON
  An ill
  illusion
Charlatan in the highest office
Hideous DEMocracy
          DEMoralizing
Are we living the lives we dreaMED of?
                Or is it full of MEDcine?
      Do we really have conTROL?
Or are we controlled by the TROLls?

✼

SILENT CURSE WORDS

They sent Jamal to detention
For saying, *erection*
Yet, Jamal saw a billboard of the
KKK with the president

Maria cried when Emily told her,
If you say f*** again, then we can't be friends
But Maria heard that they're *building a wall on CNN*

When Mohamed told Jenny, *you have a big a***
She turned and jabbed him in the face
At dinner that night Mohamed heard,
We're banning people of the Muslim faith

Danielle sat on the bench during jujitsu finals
She got a disciplinary foul for saying *you're sh*** to her rivals
But in *Time Magazine* she read,
Mississippi's refusing service to homosexuals

Ahusaka was in his room today
Tweeting to his followers about the Super Bowl
Ahusaka didn't go snowboarding today
Because he called John a *mofo*

Ding, a notification on Ahusaka's phone
From the *Chicago Tribune*
The new administration is pushing through
The pipeline under Standing Rock Sioux

Jamal, Maria, Mohamed, Danielle, and Ahusaka paid their
dues
But who will be held accountable for the *silen* curs* wor** of
the mighty few?*

MARCHING

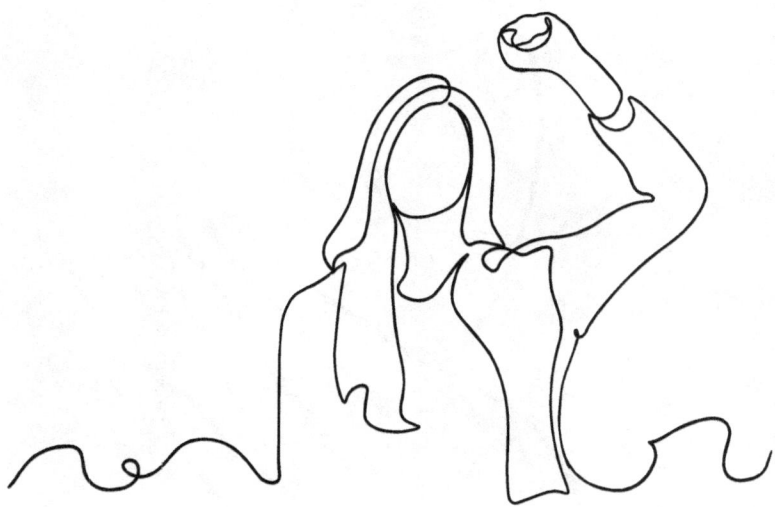

I had a dream last night
That I was
Marching
I don't know what I was marching for
or against
But I kept
Marching

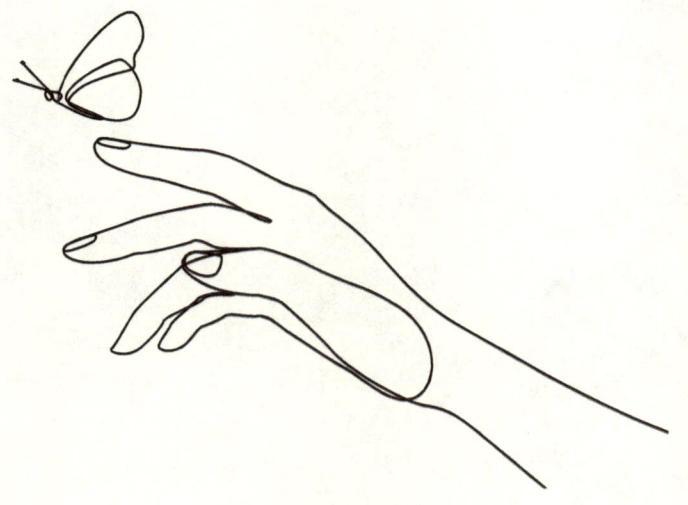

THE MOTTO

If you haven't laughed today,
you haven't lived today

HOW TO LOVE LOVE

I love love
God is made of love

So if love comes from God
Does that mean that He sends me
The love that I need?

If He sends me the love that I need
Does that mean
that each love is meant for me
Deliberately?
Intentionally?

If it's meant for me
Intentionally
Deliberately
Does that mean that its purpose
Is to heal?

And if it's a source of healing
Does that mean that I made no mistake?
By choosing the one that gave me the love

And if all this is true
Then I thank each of you
For the love that you gave me
And in this case
I don't just love love
I love the love that God gave to me

Because it heals internally
Spiritually
Eternally

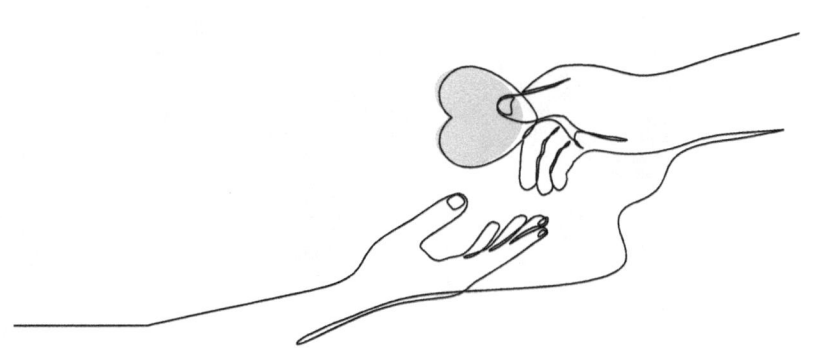

MISALIGNED

When you question
the situation, place, and decisions
that you've made

You're misaligned

When you can't breathe
a healing breath that keeps you alive

You're misaligned

When you're afraid of the now
Can't stop thinking of the how

You're misaligned

So how, you ask, Do I align?
my soul, my body, my brain?

Look in your mirror
and pray for the courage to walk away
From all that's causing you pain

Pray
to stand tall and return to your innocence
Your truth

And if you have the courage
If you stand tall
If you return
to your truth

You're aligned

�

AL SALAMU ALEIKOM

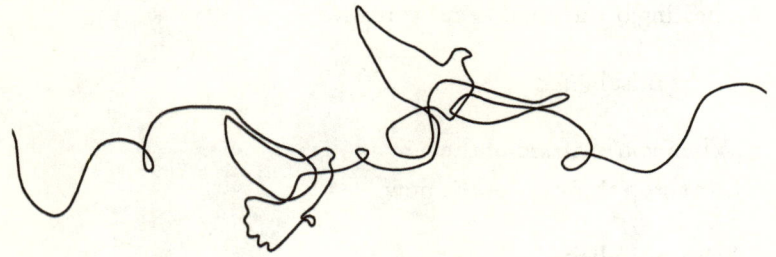

Al salamu aleikom
Wa aleikom al salam

It means peace be upon you
And peace upon you too

Now you know the meaning
of the peaceful, religious greeting

But I'm not here to preach or make you convert
I'm just here to teach you a few things that I've learned

You see, I'm sick and tired of what they tell you
How they've perfected twisting the truth

They present to you how I live my life
That I'm oppressed, one of four wives

Misinformation about Muhammad
The last of all the prophets
Peace be upon him

Yes, Muslims believe in Jesus, Moses, Joseph and Abraham
And we aspire to be like the virtuous Mariam

I bet you didn't know that cause they whisper in your ears
Spinning words and feeding you fears

Alienating and dividing you from me
Smearing the Qur'an that set me free

They don't even know Islam 101
Slaves to the dollar sign with shackled tongues

Before I go on, please answer me this
When I say Islam, what flows in your cortex?

Is it any of the four Bs?
Suicide Bombers with long, unkept Beards?
Oppressed women all in Black and filled with tears?
Belly dancers around oil-rich sheikhs?

Demonizing images they toss at you and me
Covered with the usual vocabulary,
terrorists, bombers, jihadists

Oh, those media powerhouses
They need a cure for their Alzheimer's
cause they forgot to tell you that it's a sin for me to uproot
a tree
And they forgot to tell you what jihad really means

That's why I'm here
To clear the misconceptions and correct the false
about the meaning of jihad so here it starts

An inner struggle to do what's right
Self-determination to carry your fight
Not with a weapon, but with your own moral behavior
Not with external enemies but with your inner demons

An exerted effort of improving the self
A spiritual struggle of the soul, against nobody else

Here, let me explain exactly what I mean and let's go deep
It's like when you see a woman attacked in the street
By a group of men packin' heat

Would you hide in your ride and dial 911
While they drag her on the floor taking turns one by one

This is the inner struggle in doing what's best
Even if it's against your own interests

It's like being at a concert for the late MJ
But leaving the legend cause it's time to pray

The greater jihad of fulfilling your spiritual duties
The greater jihad of serving your societies

This is the greater jihad,
the war within
Not the whack you hear on CNN

Those men with beards chanting *Allahu Akbar*
Those fundamentalists who think they're smarter

They hijacked my religion and took me as hostage
And if I don't speak the truth, I'll be one of their apostles

I'm not staying silent anymore
I'm not afraid of the political whores

. And when someone else says to you
Man, Those moozlims why they in our land?

Tell 'em, stop being such a bitch
To the media's slanderous pitch

But they fooled you and followed through
They tell us what's true and omit the truth

So it continues
Cause it's all business
And the news business is show business
And there's no business
Like show business

For the money, they've inflicted
Legitimized the opinion of the ignorant
Concealed the words of the innocent

Now go ask them
How could this be a repressive religion
when Muhammad's last words were,
Be compassionate to women

And when you hear another word
from the mouths of the herd

Straight in their eyes you look
Point at sura #5 in the sacred book

Where Allah teaches us to compete with each other
Not in wars or in killing our sisters and brothers

Sura #5 teaches us to compete in doing good
To spread moral virtues across the world

Or flip back to sura #2, right after #1
Where God tells us not to love corruption

So please, stop being so naïve
Please stop tarnishing my beliefs
Don't forget what Islam teaches, please
Don't forget the love, tolerance and peace

But if you do,
Remember what I taught you
About the greeting in Islam

Al salamu aleikom
Wa aleikom al salam

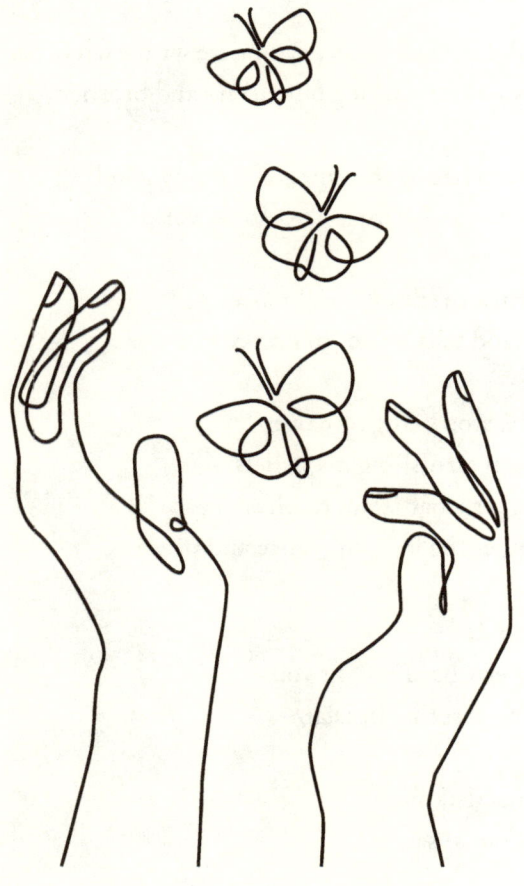

STOP AND START

Stop looking and start seeing
Stop seeing and start hearing

Stop hearing and start listening
Stop listening and start touching

Stop touching and start feeling
Stop feeling and start thinking

Stop thinking and start understanding
Stop understanding and start questioning

Stop questioning and start watching
Stop watching and start reading

Stop reading and start dancing
Stop dancing and start playing

Stop playing and start enjoying
Stop enjoying and start dreaming

Stop dreaming and . . .

No, don't stop dreaming

THE SECRET

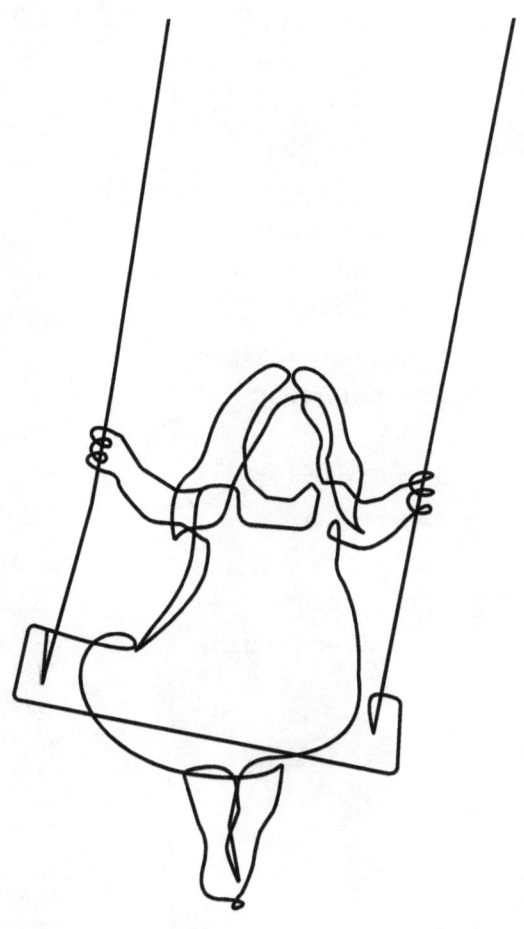

The secret to a happy life:

P

L

A

Y

ABOUT THE AUTHOR

Rasha Mohamed is an Egyptian-American writer, poet, and filmmaker. Her screenplays have won numerous awards, including The Atlanta Film Festival Screenplay Competition and Diverse Voices Screenplay Competition. Her award-winning films have screened at international film festivals, including the prestigious Cannes Film Festival. Her non-fiction book *Where are the Real Arabs and Muslims?* was the first published study that examined the portrayals and images of Muslims and Arabs in American digital news media. *Behind all The Tears* is her debut poetry book where she hand-picked a selection of poems written during her multiple lives on different lands, including California, Egypt and Dubai. She hopes that her words help readers feel seen and heard. She encourages us all to freely and proudly shed our tears—whether happy or sad—as she strongly believes in the healing powers of tears. Rasha lives in Northern California. When she's not writing, she likes to play tennis and hike the Bay Area trails.